Recession

What It Is and How It Works

Recession

What It Is and How It Works

Lisa A. Crayton and Jeanne Nagle

Enslow Publishing
101 W. 23rd Street
Suite 240
New York, NY 10011
USA
enslow.com

Published in 2016 by Enslow Publishing, LLC.
101 W. 23rd Street, Suite 240, New York, NY 10011

Library of Congress Cataloging-in-Publication Data

Names: Crayton, Lisa. | Nagle, Jeanne.
Title: Recession: what it is and how it works / Lisa A. Crayton and Jeanne Nagle.
Description: New York : Enslow Publishing, 2016. | Series: Economics in the 21st century | Includes
    bibliographical references and index.
Identifiers: ISBN 9780766073562 (library bound)
Subjects: LCSH: Recessions--United States--Juvenile literature. | Business cycles--United States--
    Juvenile literature. | Economic indicators--United States--Juvenile literature.
Classification: LCC HB3743.C685 2016 | DDC 338.5'42--dc23

Printed in the United States of America

To Our Readers: We have done our best to make sure all website addresses in this book were active and appropriate when we went to press. However, the author and the publisher have no control over and assume no liability for the material available on those websites or on any websites they may link to. Any comments or suggestions can be sent by e-mail to customerservice@enslow.com.

Portions of this text were originally written by Jeanne Nagle.

Contents

During The Great Recession (2007–2009) investors and employees were unhappy when banks like Bear Stearns failed and were sold to another bank for a fraction of their worth.

CHAPTER 1

What Is a Recession?

L earning about recession for a school project or to advance general knowledge is one thing. Living through one is something altogether different. That's what many students learned during the worst recession in the United States, appropriately dubbed "The Great Recession." That slowdown rocked the economy from December 2007, a date the National Bureau of Economic Research (NBER) identifies as the onset, through June 2009. (For more about the NBER see Chapter 3.)

Today, the effects linger for all consumers, including for Millennials, those between the ages of eighteen and thirty-four. According to a study by the Council of Economic Advisers in October 2014, the unemployment rate for Millennials was at a high point of more than 13 percent in 2010, has since fallen, but remains higher than it was prior to the Great Recession. However, a *Forbes* article noted one positive effect of the recession: it influenced Millennials' savings habits, making them more apt to invest at an earlier age than previous generations. That's an interesting fact about a recession: it generally has bad and good influences on the economy and consumers.

So, what is a recession and how does it work? This resource explores those questions and provides practical ways you can weather such economic storms. The information within these pages is designed to be a starting point for you to know more about a key economic activity. It's also a useful conversation starter to help you share your experiences with other students and adults. It can be a mutual point of connectivity to help you glean and retain knowledge that will help you better prepare for future slowdowns in the economy.

A Prosperous Start

The first years of the twenty-first century were a time of overall prosperity in the United States. A large portion of the country's population had plenty of money or were able to borrow easily from banks and other lending companies. They were not hesitant to spend what they had either. Using loans from banks and credit cards, people purchased many goods and services, especially expensive new houses.

After several years of this positive, thriving economy, however, Americans started to sense a change in the economic atmosphere. Beginning in late 2006, signs of an economic slowdown in the United States started popping up. A slowdown is when the rate of economic activity decreases. It seems that Americans had spent money faster than they could earn it. Now that the time had come to return loans and pay off credit cards, many people found themselves deeply in debt. This made it hard for them to buy anything else, so their spending decreased. Other consumers noticed this, too, and became nervous that the same thing might happen to them. Therefore, they also cut way back on their spending.

Kids are affected by recessions, too. Sometimes their music and other art classes and programs are cut when schools need to cut their budgets.

During a recession, high unemployment means people flock
to job fairs in search of work. In the meantime, they don't
have as much money to spend on necessities.

This slowdown generated many discussions in the media and debate among economists, who study the buying and selling of goods and services, about whether or not the country had entered a recession. This is when the economy experiences negative growth in total output for at least two consecutive quarters, or six months. Economists and politicians had a hard time deciding what this slowdown meant. Yet many average US citizens, who felt the effects of decreased economic activity, were certain that the country had officially entered a period of recession.

Just the idea that a recession might be looming on the horizon is enough to put people on edge. That's because there are several negative effects associated with a slowdown in economic growth. During a recession, companies sell fewer goods and services. As a result, companies lay off workers because they no longer need them. Having fewer workers also lowers a company's costs. Still, some companies go out of business. When people lose their jobs, the unemployment rate rises.

A recession is a decrease in economic activity that causes a rise in the unemployment rate. When people are not working, they are less likely to spend money on goods and services, especially luxury items. This hurts the businesses that make these goods and services. But recessions may not necessarily be a cause for concern. In fact, they are a normal part of what's known as the business cycle. The economy naturally experiences ups and downs. A recession is an example of a down period. Given time, money matters may correct themselves and start swinging back up after a slowdown.

Problems arise when the economy stays down for too long and too many people are negatively affected. When this happens, the government and businesses often give money back to citizens in the form of tax cuts, reduced interest rates on loans, or store sales. These measures are meant to help people start spending again and boost the economy back into the more healthy part of the business-cycle rhythm.

Knowing why they happen, and understanding what's likely to happen when an economic slowdown hits, can make experiencing a recession a lot less scary and getting through it a lot easier.

The Importance of Value

To understand what it means to be in a recession, it helps to understand some basic economic concepts. Economies throughout the world revolve around the idea of "value." Something is considered valuable if it is precious or special. People want or need things that are considered valuable. In economic terms, an item's value can relate to the supply and demand for the object.

When merchandise is rare or even one of a kind, like a famous artist's painting, it is considered valuable partly because there is a limited supply of this item. If an athlete is better, stronger, or faster than other players, he or she is especially valuable to the team. This will result in a great demand for the athlete and often a high salary.

The Power of Declining Value

Simply put, a recession is when the value of what a country has to offer—to its own citizens and those of other nations—decreases for at least several months. This is when a nation's economy recedes, or pulls back, from its normal buying and selling patterns. In other words, people hold back from spending as much money as they normally would or demand fewer goods and services. As a result, businesses scale back on the products they make available for sale, also known as their supply of goods and services.

Buying and selling patterns are determined primarily by examining a country's gross domestic product (GDP). This economic indicator can be calculated by adding up all the money spent on goods and services in a country. It includes products bought by households, business investments, government purchases, and net exports (goods and services sold to other countries minus the goods and services bought from other countries). All

Talented athletes, like LeBron James of the Cleveland Cavaliers, are considered valuable to the team. They are often offered a higher salary because they are in such high demand.

Cars made in the United States as well as those made internationally by American companies are included in the gross national product (GNP).

goods and services created and offered on American soil (any of the fifty states, the District of Columbia, and the five US territories) are included in the United States' GDP. Another economic statistic that refers to total output is the gross national product (GNP). The GNP measures the total amount of goods and services produced by Americans. So, this number would include cars manufactured in Detroit, Michigan, and cars produced in foreign countries by American companies.

Each nation assigns a government agency to keep track of the figures that make up the GDP. In the United States, this task is the responsibility of the

Bureau of Economic Analysis. During a recession, the numbers collected by the bureau show that the GDP is declining, or on a downward curve. This is also referred to as negative growth. When studying GDP trends, economists look at "real GDP." Nominal GDP is the number that is calculated by adding up all money spent on goods and services. Real GDP is the nominal GDP adjusted to take into account changes in the price level. By adjusting the GDP, economists can compare GDP next, without worrying that changing price levels are misrepresenting the data.

Notice that the economy needs to move downward for at least six to nine months for there to be a recession. Sometimes, the GDP numbers are low but remain flat at about the same level for months, showing no sign of moving down or up. This is a different economic phenomenon known as stagnation. Likewise, if a country experiences negative growth for only a quarter and then has positive growth the next two quarters, the economy is not considered to have been in a recession.

A Game of Dominoes

Though they often disagree on exactly when a recession has started, economists do agree on how a recession acts once it has begun. First, and most important, the rate at which people spend money slows down. This slowdown may begin in only one business sector, or field of work, at first. Eventually, the lag in spending spreads to other sectors because the economy is interdependent. That means different types of businesses are connected, so what affects one business affects many others as well.

This is called the domino effect. If you line up domino tiles and tip the first one over, it knocks over the next, which knocks over the next, and so

When one company goes out of business, workers lose their jobs; then they can't afford to spend as much. This is the domino effect at work.

on. Sectors of the economy react in much the same way during a recession. When one type of business topples, it usually shakes, and possibly completely knocks over, others.

For instance, if cars aren't selling well, then the manufacturer will not make as many vehicles. Car companies will then lay off workers because there isn't enough for them to do and because costs need to be lowered. The unemployed autoworkers no longer have enough money coming in to buy things, such as new clothes. If enough people stop buying new clothes, the clothing industry experiences a slowdown in sales. This could result in laying off more workers. A small clothing store may even lose enough sales that it is forced to go out of business, which means more people are out of a job. The more unemployed workers there are, the fewer people there are to strengthen the economy through consumer spending. This, in turn, leads to more pressure on stores and manufacturers and more layoffs. It's a vicious cycle.

Recessions Worldwide

The domino effect can be a very real factor in the world economy. Although each nation has its own financial system that is managed independently, those systems also are interdependent. This means that they rely on each other for their well-being and smooth functioning, through a process known as economic globalization. This involves connections made between businesses and marketplaces around the world. Trade (imports and exports), foreign investments, and international banking are tools of economic globalization.

Motorola Solutions, Inc. manufactures Google's Moto X smartphone
in Texas to export and be sold all over the world. Another
country's recession can mean they sell less overseas.

Just as economic slowdowns can spread from one business sector to another, a recession that starts in one country can affect the economies of financially interdependent nations. This can eventually cause a global recession. For instance, less spending in the United States doesn't lower only America's GDP. It also slows the economies of countries that export products to the United States. This is because they depend on sales to the United States to boost their own economic activity.

During a global recession, there will be a decline in the gross world product (GWP). This is the amount of all goods and services produced around the world added together. But exactly how fast and far the decline in the GWP should be to declare a global recession hasn't been established. The International Monetary Fund (IMF), a financial monitoring organization, estimates that the global economy (as measured by the GWP) would grow by only 3 percent or less during a worldwide recession. According to the IMF's measurement, the last global recession occurred in 2001–2002.

Hills and Valleys

What many people don't realize is that recessions are a normal part of the way the economy works. The movement of the economy is called the business cycle. If you were to make a chart showing economic activity over the course of a year, it would look like a wavy line or a small mountain range, complete with hills and valleys. That's because the business cycle goes through a series of ups, called peaks, and downs, known as troughs. When the cycle is on its way up, the economy is experiencing more growth than usual. It is said to be going through an expansion. The economy is said to go through a contraction when it is on its way down. The contractions that happen during the normal business cycle are actually recessions.

In a way, contractions are how the economy cools itself down after it has heated up and expanded too much. Expansions, likewise, are how the economy recovers and climbs back up after experiencing a trough. The economy works best when it has this fluid, moderate up-and-down motion. It is as if constantly changing creates a kind of balance and stability.

Over the course of a normal business cycle, the contractions, or recessions, usually are not too severe, and they correct themselves fairly quickly. According to the National Bureau of Economic Research (NBER), recessions generally last, on average, about a year.

Defining Recession and Depression

Within the business cycle, a depression is more than a contraction. It is most definitely a trough. A depression is a major economic decline, where people struggle to pay for the basic necessities of life, such as food and shelter.

Economists use the GDP to help gauge whether a slowdown is a recession or a depression. A decline of less than 10 percent in the GDP is considered a recession.

In the 1970s, the United States economy experienced a slowdown that economists now agree was a true recession. Over two years, from 1973 to 1975, the country's GDP fell nearly 5 percent. A 10 percent decrease in the GDP signals a depression. During the well-known Great Depression—one of the darkest times in United States economic history that lasted throughout the 1930s—the GDP dropped about 30 percent at its lowest point. Even as

During a depression, people might struggle to buy even the most basic things. If times get extremely tough, they may lose their homes and seek help in a shelter.

the economy was working its way out of trouble, the decline in the GDP stayed above the 10 percent threshold.

Recessions and depressions are related in that they are both part of the downward curve of the business cycle. The difference is that recessions aren't as deep or long-lived as depressions. Also, while recessions always come before depressions, because the economy can't jump right from a peak to a deep trough, not all recessions turn into depressions.

Myths and Facts About Recessions

Myth: The business cycle is a fairly regular series of economic ups and downs.

Fact: The business cycle does show peaks and troughs in the economy, but it is by no means regular or consistent. Recessions can be lengthy or short, as can the time between them. That's why recessions are so hard to predict.

Myth: The stock market is the most important indicator in determining whether or not the country is in a recession.

Fact: Watching the stock market is helpful in that it reflects economic health and consumer confidence, but it is not the most important indicator. A nation's GDP and employment rate give a much better overall picture of an economic slowdown.

Myth: Recessions are disastrous for the economy.

Fact: How negatively a recession affects the economy depends on how long and deep it is. Over the past twenty years, recessions have been relatively short and mild. In between those troughs, the United States experienced great growth. Recessions can be merely the economy balancing itself after extreme growth, rather than signaling a crisis or disaster.

CHAPTER 2

What Causes Recession?

An airline announces a forty-eight-hour price drop for travel to select cities and advertises the deal online. Word quickly spreads through social media, and the company's website crashes because of the number of people trying to access the website and grab the deal before it skyrockets back up. In the music world, a pop singer announces on a TV news show that she is releasing a new single. Its price of 99 cents on iTunes attracts attention from fans all around the world. Within hours, the single hits never-before-reached sales levels. In another area of the economy, a hamburger chain launches a new line of salads to attract customers who like healthy choices. In a few months that changes. Soft sales result in the chain pulling the salads off its menu.

What is happening in each situation? The law of supply and demand is affecting the economy. The world of economics is ruled by this "law" based upon typical economic activity that maps how buyers and sellers act on their own and react to each other.

Supply and demand also have a direct effect on the business cycle. The relationship between the availability of products and people wanting to purchase those goods and services is responsible for the business cycle's

If an airline advertises a great, limited-time deal on certain
flights (supply), demand will likely increase as people rush
to order tickets while this enticing offer lasts.

expansions and contractions. That connection, along with both unwelcome interruptions, known as "shocks," and the way a nation's government handles its money supply, can ultimately determine whether or not a country experiences a recession.

Marketplace Changes

The law of supply and demand states that the value of a good or service changes according to how much of that given product is available (the supply) as well as how much people want it (demand). Supply and demand influence the price people pay for goods and services in the marketplace.

For instance, if the supply of a product, or the amount available, is high, then the product is not rare. Remember, value is connected to how rare or precious something is. Consequently, the item's price will be low when its supply, or availability, is high. Likewise, the price of an item increases when it is in short supply.

Also, the more popular or useful an item is, the more people will demand it. Initially, the high demand will result in a short supply of the product. Think about the long lines of hopeful customers that formed outside of electronics and computer stores when the latest versions of PlayStation, Nintendo Wii, or the iPhone were released. Many people went home empty handed. When that happens, a business eventually increases production to meet the growing demand.

Increased production comes at a cost, though. Companies need to hire more workers and use more materials as they boost their supplies by making more products. To get back some of the money they're spending on additional employee wages and extra materials, businesses often mark up the price of their merchandise. This helps them make a profit. Money earned from the sale of a product beyond what it costs to create and sell that product is called profit. As long as production costs go up, prices typically will go up as well.

Depending on how strong the demand for goods and services is, and how much money customers can earn or borrow to pay for their purchases, everything may run smoothly in this way for months or even years. Yet, true to the law of supply and demand, higher prices eventually result in decreased demand for a good or service because many people will be either unable or unwilling to pay the higher price.

In 2007, gas prices started to soar. By July 17, gas was selling at its highest level ever—$4.11 per gallon. People responded by lowering their demand for gas. Rather than drive their own cars, people took public transportation, walked, or joined a carpool. By October, demand had decreased by 10 percent compared to the previous year. Less demand caused gas prices to drop, and on October 7, 2008, gas was selling for $3.48 per gallon.

Balance Restored

When demand for goods and services goes down, the marketplace tries to restore balance by slowing down or contracting. Prices drop, and items go on sale in the hope of selling off the supply that has built up when demand was high. Production slows down. However, there are some areas of the economy that resist quick correction. Some costs of doing business remain high even as the rest of the economy contracts. These areas are said to be "sticky" because during periods of economic contraction, they get stuck at expansion levels.

Wages and income are examples of this "stickiness." Workers are hired at salary levels that reflect the current economy. If an expansion is under way, then starting wages will be higher than normal. When a slowdown occurs, businesses might offer lower salaries to new employees, but wages for those who are already employed do not automatically go down. People keep earning the salary that was agreed upon when they were first hired. Companies are more likely to lay off workers than try to reduce sticky wages.

Another example of economic stickiness concerns so-called menu costs. The best example of this type of stickiness is the price list on restaurant menus. Once prices are set and put into a printed, semipermanent form, such as on menus or in brochures, businesses cannot easily change them to reflect an economic contraction. The cost of redoing printed materials every time the economy changes would cause more damage to a business than simply leaving prices high.

Sticky wages and prices that cannot drop as fast as the economy contracts put a serious glitch in the business cycle. They can result in not hiring workers or laying off workers, which can worsen the economic contraction.

System Shocks

Sometimes, the economy can be performing well and expanding when suddenly a major event comes along that throws the business cycle off course, pushing a country toward recession. These events, called economic shocks, include natural disasters, such as hurricanes and earthquakes; armed conflicts and wars; the introduction of expensive government programs; and difficulty obtaining nonrenewable natural resources, such as oil.

When shocks occur, money that normally would build up a nation's economy is instead spent taking care of issues surrounding the event. For example, in 2005, Hurricane Katrina devastated New Orleans and much

Hurricane Katrina was a severe economic shock
when it ravaged New Orleans and parts of the Gulf Coast,
costing more than $81 million in damages and shocking the economy.

of the Gulf Coast, resulting in 1,836 deaths and an estimated $81.2 billion in damage. The US government had to aid in the cleanup and recovery using funds that it raised through taxes and donations from average citizens. Disaster and humanitarian relief is necessary spending, yet it comes at a steep cost. When money is used for economic shocks, it is not used for something else. It's as if you were saving for an iPod but then your car broke down, so you had to sink all of your savings into auto repairs instead.

Understanding Inflation

It might be hard to understand how having more money in circulation could cause a slowdown in the economy, but it's true. The law of supply and demand affects cold, hard cash as much as any other good or service. So, the more money that is in circulation—meaning spread out among the public—the less valuable each bill and coin becomes because of the high supply. When money becomes less valuable, it takes more of it to buy stuff. This is inflation—a time when there's plenty of money to go around, but it doesn't buy as much as it once did.

Inflation means that prices rise to make up for the value of money going down. An item may be worth one dollar, but a dollar bill has dropped in value and is now worth only fifty cents. Therefore, it takes two dollar bills (each worth one dollar before inflation) to buy the item now. This 50 percent inflation rate has raised the price of a one-dollar product to two dollars, while each of those dollars can buy only half of what they used to. Each dollar has lost half of its former purchasing power.

Governments are primarily responsible for bringing about inflation, which makes trouble for their own economies. Just like individual citizens, countries must have cash to pay for the things they need, including roads and

During a recession, prices go up as the value of money goes down, so
the money in your wallet doesn't buy you as much as it once did.

bridges, education, research, and programs such as Medicare and homeland
security. Unlike ordinary people, however, the federal government has a
great deal of control over its money supply. When a nation runs short on
money, the government can simply print and stamp more. The government
inflates, or increases, the money supply to meet its needs. This trick doesn't
last long, though, because eventually the law of supply and demand catches
up with the government, in the form of inflation. The more money that
gets printed, the less each bill is worth.

Economic Benefits of War

Throughout history, wars have been known to stimulate, or speed up, the economy instead of slowing it down. In fact, many historians believe that military spending during World War II helped the United States rebound from that ultimate economic slowdown, the Great Depression.

Oddly enough, wars can be good for the economy, at least in their early stages. Feeding, clothing, and otherwise taking care of the troops pumps money into a nation's GDP. Manufacturing and purchasing weapons creates jobs in the industrial and defense sectors. Over time, however, conflicts can be a drain on the economy. The money being spent on defense costs gets siphoned away from other areas of the economy and business sectors. Sometimes, governments even have to borrow money from other countries to be able to continue to pay their war expenses. This increases their national debt and puts a further break on other kinds of spending that could stimulate the economy and head off a recession.

Consumer Response to Price Hikes

Inflation's effect on a recession has a lot to do with the behavior of consumers in response to rising prices. Some people will slow down their spending pretty quickly because items are too expensive. Others will keep buying products no matter what the cost because there is a large supply of money

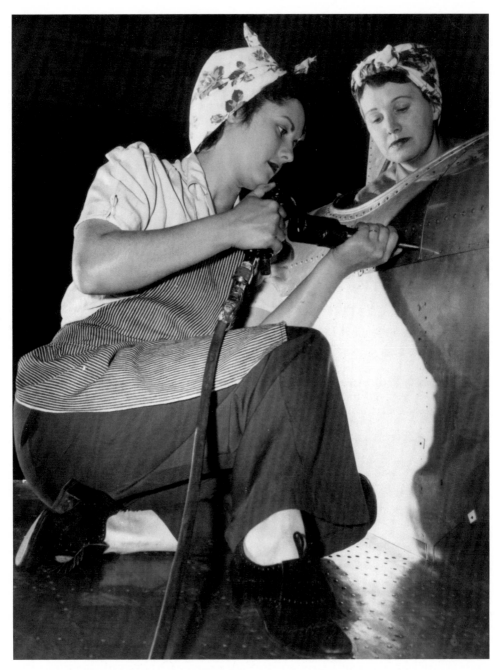

Believe it or not, the early stages of war are very good for an economy. For example, jobs are created to manufacture and purchase weapons.

Consumers are likely to reduce or stop buying luxury items, such as expensive cars, during a recession. They tend to use their money to buy necessities instead.

still available to them—either through wages that have risen to reflect the higher cost of living or through banks with plenty of cash to lend.

Eventually, however, inflation causes people to pull back on spending, mostly because their wages can't keep up with rising prices. Less spending creates a contraction in the business cycle, and the economy cools off and slows down.

If you want to keep a close eye on the health of your economy, you can get apps for your smartphone that will send you almost instant updates.

CHAPTER 3

Recession's Red Flags

D ependable economic information is readily available from newspapers, magazines, and books (including e-books), as well as on television and on the Internet. It is also possible to get instant updates from smartphone apps. Those data are helpful in predicting and identifying a recession. But how does the average person make sense of all the facts and figures?

One of the best methods is to listen to what the experts have to say. Such experts exist in the public, private, and government sectors. Their job is to analyze various economic indicators and come to conclusions about how the economy is faring at any given time. They are "big picture" experts who look at short- and long-term effects of economic indicators and share their predictions about if and when a recession will occur. Even if they don't agree on all the details, they are generally in sync when it comes to the big picture and the main ideas behind recessions.

You can also watch for signs of a slowdown yourself, as you may have discovered during the Great Recession. There are a number of economic indicators, or markets, that can act as red flags, warning you that a recession is coming or has already arrived. Some consumers rather adopt a "wait-and-see" attitude to economic activity. The Great Recession, however, proved the importance of predicting and identifying a recession. By listening and watching, you'll have a better idea of the economic situation in the world at large and in your own life.

America's Central Bank

When it comes to national money matters, the Federal Reserve is the recognized authority within the United States. The Federal Reserve, often referred to simply as the Fed, is the country's central bank. The federal government and all other financial institutions in America use the Fed as their bank, just like you use the local branch of your bank. The central bank gets most of its money from interest earned on government securities, including US savings bonds and treasury bills. In 2005, this amount totaled $28.96 billion. The Federal Reserve also receives money from interest earned on foreign investments and on loans to banks, as well as services provided to other banks, such as check clearing. The Fed turns all its money over to the US Treasury for safekeeping, minus its operating expenses.

An independent organization that operates within the United States government but is not considered a government agency, the Fed is watched over by the US Congress and run by a board that is appointed by the president. As part of its job, the board analyzes the economy and makes policy recommendations. As head of the board, the Fed chairman delivers a report on the state of the economy to Congress twice a year.

The Fed's job is to oversee the country's banking operations and make sure that the economy stays healthy. It does this by trying to ensure that

The US Treasury Building is located in Washington DC. This is where the Federal Reserve places most of its money for safekeeping.

overall demand equals potential supply within the economy. Therefore, it does not so much determine whether a recession has begun as try to keep normal business cycle contractions as short as possible.

To accomplish this, the Fed uses interest rates. During periods of rising inflation, the Fed can raise interest rates to keep the economy in check. And during economic contractions, such as a recession, the Fed lowers interest rates. Lower rates essentially mean it costs less to borrow money. With low interest rates, the fee for borrowing money is less. The hope is that consumers will feel more comfortable taking out loans at low interest rates, and they will then use that money to boost the economy in the form of spending.

Countries around the world have similar national organizations that influence their business cycles. The Bank of Canada, the People's Bank of China, and the European Central Bank (representing countries in the financially linked European Union) are all examples of international institutions that have duties and powers like those of the US Federal Reserve.

NBER's Influence

The Fed has control over interest rates, and the United States government determines how much of the country's money is printed. Both of these acts affect contractions in the business cycle. However, the task of declaring a recession is typically left to a well-respected, privately owned, nonprofit organization called the National Bureau of Economic Research (NBER).

The NBER has built a solid reputation as a knowledgeable, influential force when it comes to shaping American economic policy and programs.

Signs of the Times

What visible signs of struggle or recovery are identifiable during an economy's normal business cycles? Three common ones are as follows:

Job postings. "We're hiring. Inquire Within" signs at retail stores, fast food restaurants, and other business show that more jobs are available. The reverse happens during a recession: retail stores, restaurants, and other employers stop hiring, lay off workers, or close.

Wages. Employers adjust wages during a recession to avoid cutting jobs, so a wage freeze or reduction is one way to know that the economy is declining. During an upturn, employers increase wages through raises and bonuses.

"We are hiring" signs show that the economy is on an upswing. Businesses need more employees to fill more available positions.

Cost shifts. During a recession employers may shift increased cost of health insurance to the employee. During a recovery, employers may take on more costs by offering employees more paid time off or increase the amount of money it matches for each dollar an employee saves in 401(k) plans.

Economists keep an eye on the number of new houses built in a month
or a quarter to gauge how well the economy is growing or slowing.

Most-Watched Indicators

- **Gross domestic product (GDP)**—Perhaps the most reliable leading indicator, the GDP reveals overall buying and selling patterns on a monthly, quarterly, or yearly basis and moves in the same direction as the business cycle. Therefore, during an economic contraction, the GDP decreases.

- **Unemployment figures**—A lagging indicator, unemployment numbers reflect entry into a recession but do not predict one.

- **Stock market**—Declining stock prices may signal an upcoming recession. Therefore, the performance of stock indices, like the Dow Jones Industrial Average or the Standard & Poor's 500, can be a leading indicator.

- **Consumer price index (CPI)**—A coincident indicator, the CPI tracks what customers are paying for goods and services.

- **Housing starts**—A leading indicator, this statistic measures the number of new homes that are built within a specific period, usually a month or a quarter.

- **Consumer confidence**—This leading indicator gauges how people feel about the economy and the security of their income, based on a survey of five thousand households. Low consumer confidence predicts a reduction in consumer spending.

In fact, the federal government looks to the bureau's Business Cycle Dating Committee to make the official determination as to whether or not a recession has taken place. The committee checks the economic situation on a monthly basis, not quarterly as other organizations do.

While paying close attention to the GDP, the committee also considers income, employment, and industrial production figures before announcing that the economy is in recession. Using these economic indicators, the committee identifies when the business cycle has peaked and exactly when it has hit a trough. The time between those two high and low points is what the NBER calls a recession.

Clues to the Economy

To reach its conclusions regarding a recession, the NBER looks at sets of collected information known as economic indicators. They are called this because the data and statistics indicate, or point out, the direction of the economy.

You might think that when a slowdown is involved, indicators would also show a decline. But, this is not always the case. Economic indicators can be either procyclic or countercyclic. Procyclic indicators move in the same direction as the business cycle. During a recession, these statistics move downward along with the economy. Retail sales are an example of procyclic indicators. If sales figures are up, then the economy is expanding. When they fall, there is an economic contraction.

Credible Economic Indicators

Not all collections of economic indicators are created equal. Several groups publish indicator lists, but the most trusted source for reliable data in America is the Joint Economic Committee (JEC) of the US Congress. The committee is made up of twenty members—ten senators and ten members of the House of Representatives, from both major political parties.

Working with the Council of Economic Advisers—a group of economists who give input to the president on economic policy—the JEC analyzes indicators each month in seven categories. These are total output, income, and spending; employment, unemployment, and wages; production and business activity; prices; money, credit, and security markets; federal finance; and international statistics.

Another respected collection of economic statistics is the Index of Leading Economic Indicators (LEI). Compiled by the Conference Board, a nonprofit business research organization established in 1916, the LEI measures the business-cycle changes in nine countries, including the United States. The index factors in many things, including the average hours worked each week by manufacturing employees and the number of orders they fill to the performance of the stock market and how confident consumers are in the health of their national economies.

Altogether, the LEI's indicators reflect all GDP-influencing factors. If the leading indicators show a decline for three consecutive months, within the next year the economy is likely to enter a recession.

Ancient Romans' failed attempts to improve their economy included shaving the edges off their silver denarius and melting the shavings into new coins. They also tried mixing in other metals.

CHAPTER 4
Recessions in the Real World

Trust is important to the running of an economy. Consumers must trust merchants and vice versa. The absence of trust tanks supply and demand, making it more difficult for successful trade. Money itself may also take a hard hit as people begin to wonder if its value is sufficient to cover the cost of a good or service.

A healthy money supply leads to a healthy economy. When money supply is low, governments intervene. That's what the ancient Roman government did, but its efforts backfired. Rather than actually making more money, the government tried to increase its supply by shaving silver from the edges of the denarius, which was the empire's coin money. The shavings were melted and made into new coins. Neither the original shaved coins nor the new ones contained as much silver as they should have, however, so the denarius literally lost a chunk of its value. The empire also tried mixing metals that weren't as precious as silver into coins, which made the denarius worth less as well.

The people of Rome started getting wise to what was happening. Merchants didn't trust the value of the denarius, so they started charging more for goods and services. Because there was so much devalued money circulating in the Roman economy, prices rose and the empire experienced inflation. The typical citizen's supply of money could not keep up with the increasing cost of living.

Modern recessions haven't necessarily gone so far as to topple empires, but they have caused major disruptions to the normal business cycle, seriously harmed nations' fortunes, and affected millions of people.

Panic of 1819

The first major economic slowdown in America, known as the Panic of 1819, came after a period of expansion that followed the War of 1812. At that time, the country was filled with land speculators. These were men who borrowed money from banks and bought acreage so they could break the land into smaller lots and sell them quickly to make a profit. If the speculators didn't sell the land, there was a chance that the banks would not get back the money that they had given out as loans.

To buy the land, speculators took out loans from state and local banks. The Bank of the United States—which was the country's central bank at the time, an early version of the Federal Reserve—wanted to prevent state banks from making any more of these risky loans. As a result, it called in loans that it had made to the smaller banks. Without funds from the central bank, the state banks were forced to demand payment from the speculators on the credit and mortgage loans that had been given to them. Speculators who had not sold their landholdings could not make these payments. Many people lost their homes and were wiped out financially.

On top of the loan crisis, American exports, especially cotton to England, had declined rapidly. Other nations stopped buying US goods, and Americans couldn't afford to buy much either. The slowdown in buying and selling

On top of the loan crisis, cotton exports to England quickly
plummeted during the Panic of 1819. US goods, like those
made out of cotton, weren't purchased overseas.

created a recession. What followed were five years of massive unemployment, bank closings, and a drastic slowdown in the manufacturing and agriculture business sectors.

Hard Times Persist

Over the next century, the United States went through several additional recessions, including a downturn at the end of World War I in 1918. The economy soon rebounded after that, however. A strong business-cycle expansion took over during the first half of the appropriately nicknamed Roaring Twenties.

Even in the middle of this prosperity, though, there were troubling signs of economic problems in the United States. People and businesses borrowed heavily so they could spend lavishly. They also sank money into risky stock market investments. Consequently, money that should have been used to buy new items was instead spent on paying off debt or was lost entirely because of bad investments. By the mid-1920s, the country's GDP was shrinking, especially in the sectors of housing and durable goods (things like cars, appliances, furniture, and office equipment). American farmers also fell on hard times because there wasn't a strong demand for their products overseas. Without the income from exported food, many farmers couldn't afford to pay the mortgages on their land and homes.

All of these things contributed to the recession that eventually turned into the Great Depression, which began in 1929. For ten years, the world remained in this business-cycle trough.

Military spending and increased industrial output in Europe and the United States at the start of World War II are largely credited with putting an end to the depression.

When Less Is More

In the aftermath of the Great Recession, one term is still being used to reflect consumers' desire to prepare for the future by reducing their overall debt or limiting the amount of personal items they possess. That term is *downsizing*. There is no one-size-fits-all strategy for downsizing. Some homeowners have downsized by selling larger homes and moving into smaller ones to reduce mortgage debt and free up cash for future savings and investments.

How can you downsize? It makes sense to start with those possessions that are in good condition but rarely used—such as clothing, video games, and household items. Donate those to charitable organizations or give to needy families.

Personal downsizing is simple. Donate clothes or other items that are in good shape but are just sitting around unused to the needy or other charities.

Triple Threats

After two minor slowdowns in the 1950s, recessions in America have occurred roughly every ten years. Each has lasted anywhere from a few months to two years. The first in this series, a two-year recession that began in 1973, was the result of several factors. It was sparked by international political disagreements and a subsequent economic shock in the form of an oil shortage.

A group of predominantly Arab nations were part of an oil-producing alliance known as OPEC (Organization of Petroleum Exporting Countries). OPEC was, and remains, one of the main suppliers of the oil that is consumed in the United States. OPEC placed an embargo on the United States (an embargo is when trading with another nation is forbidden). The embargo completely shut off the sale of oil to the United States.

The lack of imported oil from the Middle East greatly reduced the nation's supply of petroleum products, such as heating fuel and gasoline. People had to wait in long lines at gas stations. For a while, gas was rationed, meaning customers could buy only so many gallons during each trip to the pump. Because oil was now precious, its value rose, as did its price. Inflation took over. Money that should have been boosting the GDP through purchases in lots of different business sectors was instead being used to fill automobile and truck gas tanks and heat people's houses and businesses. When combined with years of heavy military spending on the war in Vietnam and higher than normal unemployment before the embargo, increasing prices soon drove the US economy into a recession.

Cars in Brooklyn, New York, are lined up to get gas, which
was scarce during the recession that started in 1973. Gas
became expensive because it was in short supply.

Bank Crisis Levels S&Ls

The late 1980s and early 1990s were an active, complex time for the US economy. The country was dealing with a banking crisis, when hundreds of small savings and loan banks (known as S&Ls) were failing, or going out of business, because of corruption and having made too many bad loans. America was also shaken by Black Monday on October 19, 1987, when the stock market experienced one of the largest single-day drops in history. Black Monday affected stock trading around the world.

Strangely enough, these events rattled the US economy but did not immediately cause a recession. It would not be until almost three years later that the economy officially entered a recession. According to the Business Cycle Dating Committee, the 1990–1991 economic downturn was caused by a decrease in manufacturing production and sales—one of the components of the GDP. Recall that the GDP is the total value of all goods and services produced in the country in a given period.

The committee also noted dips in personal income and an increase in unemployment figures, but these indicators hadn't experienced clear troughs like the manufacturing numbers had.

Dot-Coms Bomb

After the 1990–1991 recession, the US economy experienced renewed expansion. It was being driven mainly by what was then a new business sector—Internet-based companies. Existing "brick-and-mortar" retail businesses found they could increase their sales by using advanced technology and the World Wide Web. They would sell their wares on the Web, in addition to or in place of traditional buying and selling in physical stores.

On October 19, 1987, a day that would become known as
Black Monday, the stock market dropped more than any other
day in history. Brokers and investors were devastated.

Buying and selling online became popular. Hoping to take advantage of this situation and make a lot of money, businesspeople created hundreds of companies that specialized exclusively in online sales and computer technology. These were known as dot-coms because the new companies often had ".com" at the end of their names, which is Internet shorthand for "commerce."

Many investors bought stock in these new ventures. They were speculating that dot-coms would make large profits, causing their stock value to increase as well. Heavy investing created what is known as a stock bubble, where the price of stock in a certain business sector rises rapidly, sometimes regardless of the company's actual worth or the value of its products. The increased demand for the stock inflates the value of the stock and the perceived value and health of the company. In their rush to make money, the owners of many dot-coms hadn't created good business plans or even created any actual products to sell. They were simply selling the promise of a product that would eventually be offered and sold. Many of these companies built on flimsy foundations soon folded. Also, there were too many Internet-based companies on the market at one time, and there wasn't enough business to support them all. The supply of dot-coms far exceeded demand for their services, so company values declined. By 2001, the technology stock bubble had burst. Stock prices fell, spending decreased, and many more Internet companies went out of business. The result was a stock market drop, a declining GDP, and an increase in unemployment figures as thousands of dot-com workers lost their jobs.

The recession that followed was also affected by the shock of the September 11 terrorist attacks on New York and Washington, DC in 2001. Even after all this upheaval, though, the slowdown was relatively mild and, according to the NBER, lasted only eight months.

Housing and Credit Woes

In the early years of the twenty-first century, many Americans took advantage of low interest rates—which had been cut by the Fed to help kick-start the economy after the 2001 recession—to take out loans, especially home mortgages. Knowing they could collect more money if they made more loans at lower interest rates, banks also lowered their mortgage interest rates and lending requirements. They even made subprime loans to people who were bad credit risks, although at higher interest rates. "Subprime" means that the borrower does not have a good credit rating and the loan is far riskier than an ordinary loan. Subprime loans used to be avoided or were carefully insured in case the borrower could not pay back the loan. In the 2000s, however, subprime loans increased dramatically.

It became so easy to buy real estate that everyone wanted in on the action. Buyers also took advantage of the "easy money" banks were offering by using their homes as collateral to borrow even more money to make other big-ticket purchases (such as second homes, boats, or luxury cars). Collateral is valuable property that a borrower agrees to give to a lender if payments are not made on a loan. The value of houses went up as the demand increased, as did real estate prices. Unfortunately, personal income didn't rise to the same level. Soon, houses cost more than the average consumer could afford. By 2007, home sales dropped and borrowers defaulted on loans, meaning they failed to pay them back on time.

After 2001, banks offered subprime loans. Many couldn't keep up
with their payments, defaulted on their loans, and had to foreclose
on their houses. All this helped trigger another recession.

Complicating matters was the fact that groups of risky subprime mortgages were offered as a special kind of investment opportunity, known as securities. Basically, outside investors gave banks the funds to cover these shaky loans, expecting in return to share the money from interest when the loans were repaid. When subprime borrowers defaulted, the investors lost money along with the banks. This caused a shake-up in stock markets worldwide, because international banks and investors had purchased these securities. Even those investors who had stayed away from the securities became nervous because they were afraid their stocks and other investments would fail just like the subprime securities had. As a result, they made fewer new investments, even in relatively safe and healthy companies and projects.

Several indicators seemed to suggest that the economy was in a recession after these housing and credit difficulties. Stock market trading and the GDP dropped. Jobs were cut in the real estate, construction, and finance sectors, so unemployment rose. Yet, by the second half of 2008, the slowdown hadn't met either the two-consecutive-quarters or the NBER's "several months" definition of a recession. There was no arguing with one important indicator, though. Consumer confidence was low. A majority of the American public believed that they were in the middle of a recession, and they were no longer spending their money. Finally, in November 2008, consumers' suspicions were confirmed. The United States—along with several other nations—was declared to have officially entered a recessionary period, one that was expected to be both deep and long-lasting.

10 Great Questions to Ask a Financial Adviser

- What state is the economy in now, and how do you, personally, determine that?

- Given my income and expenses, how tight should my budget be?

- How much money should I be saving each month? What percentage of my income should be set aside?

- What form of savings is going to earn the most interest?

- When is the best time for me to make major purchases?

- What types of payment plans would you suggest for clearing up credit card debt?

- What business sectors offer the most job security during a recession?

- What investment strategy do you recommend during an economic slowdown?

- What advice have you given clients in the past that they say has helped them the most?

- How can I best plan for my financial future five, ten, twenty years down the road?

CHAPTER 5
Coping With Recession

When an economy has retracted, citizens are wary of any fluctuations in the business cycle. When they are still coping with effects from a previous downturn, those consumers may worry about how to deal with the effects of any pending recession. One of the first steps is the acknowledgement that recession is inevitable simply because it is a normal part of the business cycle. The fact is, as part of that cycle, recessions occur in the United States, on average every five to ten years. Given that schedule, learning to cope with recession is a must.

You can be better prepared if you know when a recession might happen. Predicting a recession is tricky business. The National Bureau of Economic Research (NBER) states that in recent years, economic slowdowns have been cropping up less frequently than in decades past. According to Kenneth Rogoff of the International Monetary Fund, global recessions occur about as often, every eight to ten years. Beyond these facts, however, no one can be certain when the business cycle will contract or how difficult a given contraction may be.

To be prepared for an economic slowdown, families can budget carefully to make sure they are not spending more money than they are bringing in.

So how can governments and individuals prepare for a recession? By recognizing that these economic slowdowns are unavoidable, but suffering through them is not. Governments can introduce measures aimed at minimizing the effects of a recession before it starts while making sure that their own actions regarding the economy do not get out of control. Citizens should pay close attention to the law of supply and demand in their own lives. They can try their best to live within their means—and encourage their government and elected officials to do the same. Both governments and ordinary citizens can best fight a recession by remaining calm, careful, and reasonable in their actions and reactions.

Economic Policy

Economic policy is an attempt by a nation's government or central bank to influence the movements of the business cycle. Policy is meant to be an intervention measure—getting involved in a positive way—rather than interference, which is negative and blocks progress.

There are two categories of policy that directly affect the economy: fiscal policy and monetary policy. Fiscal policy is the responsibility of lawmakers and other government officials. In the United States, this includes the president and Congress. With fiscal policy, the government adds money to the economy to increase the demand for goods and services. The thinking is that people will spend more when there is more money available to them, thereby stimulating and expanding the economy.

Reducing taxes and increasing government spending are the two main fiscal policies that are used to insert money into the economy. Lowering

Road construction might slow you down on your way to the movies, but it helps kick-start the economy by creating jobs, for example.

the amount paid in taxes—through yearly income tax filings or sales tax on purchases—leaves more money available to spend in taxpayers' pockets. Tax rebates, in which the government sends checks to taxpayers as a way to get them to spend more, may also occur during a recession. This tactic was tried in 2001 and, most recently, in 2008.

Government spending, either directly on goods and services or through projects such as road and bridge construction, stimulates the economy in a different way. Government spending jump-starts production in various business sectors, creating more jobs and greater demand for goods and services. Money makes its way back into the economy through increased GDP and personal income.

Understanding Subsidies

When a company is unable to make a profit, it is discouraging for that business's owner and its employees. When whole groups of companies in a particular business sector don't turn a profit, it is bad news for the entire economy. When this happens, the government turns to a form of spending known as subsidies.

A subsidy is a government payment meant to encourage economic activity in a business or business sector that provides a necessary or unique product. When lack of profit threatens such an industry (like agriculture, steel, or automobile manufacturing), the government supports, or subsidizes, it with cash. This helps lower production costs and keeps the various companies within the industry in business.

Sometimes in a industry like farming it is difficult to make a profit, so the government steps in with assistance, called subsidies, to help keep the farmer in business.

Tools for Monetary Policy

Monetary policy is the responsibility of a country's central bank, which in the United States is the Federal Reserve. The goal of monetary policy is to stabilize employment levels and prices by influencing the availability of money and the affordability of borrowing and credit. To accomplish this, more money needs to be injected into the economy.

The Fed has three major tools that help set monetary policy in motion. Open market operations involve the buying and selling of government securities such as bonds and treasury bills (T-bills). Citizens buy these bonds and bills with the government's promise that, after holding on to them for a certain period of time, they will be worth more than the original price paid. It's like buying stock, only you're investing in the government instead of an individual company. Because they are backed by the US government, bonds and T-bills are considered safe investments. The money that the government raises by selling securities can be spent on all kinds of programs that would otherwise have to be funded by the raising of taxes.

During a recession, the government may buy back the securities it has sold, kind of like paying off an I.O.U. with interest. The money the government pays goes directly to the person who bought the securities. Most people will spend at least some of the money they earn from the sale of their securities back to the government, thus pumping much-needed money back into the economy.

Bonds and Treasury bills are backed by the US government and are considered safe investments. The Fed sells these to set monetary policy in motion.

DAILY NEWS

Copr. 1946 by News Syndicate Co. Inc. NEW YORK'S PICTURE NEWSPAPER   Trade Mark Reg. U. S. Pat. Off.

FINAL

Vol. 28   No. 96   New York 17, Tuesday, October 15, 1946*   48 Pages   2 Cents IN CITY LIMITS | 3 CENTS In Suburbs | 5 CENTS Elsewhere

MEAT CONTROLS
TAKEN OFF

Truman Ends Price Curbs;
Other Ceilings Stay for Now

——Story on Page 3

'There Is Only One Remedy Left'

(Associated Press Wirefoto)

With this declaration, President Truman, talking to the nation last night, ordered all price controls on meat lifted today. If you are thinking of rushing out for a steak, though, better slow down to a walk; it'll be weeks yet.

Joyful News comes to Mrs. Rose Cali and her children in home at 58 E. Third St., as she scans headline of one of first editions of the News carrying Truman's speech and sees a chance of replenishing the empty refrigerator. —*Story on page 8*

(NEWS foto by Reuss)

Sometimes price controls are set on necessities to keep their prices from rising above a limit. But this is problematic for manufacturers when their expenses are still rising.

Another monetary policy tool is a reduced interest rate on loans from the Fed to other banks. This is known as discount window lending because there is an actual teller's window at the Fed that other banks use when taking out discounted loans. It's similar to the commercial transactions window set aside for businesses at your local bank branch.

When the country is in a recession, the Fed wants to encourage borrowing from any source. Cutting interest rates on loans is one way to entice individuals, businesses, and even other banks to obtain credit and increase their ability to spend or invest. When the Fed cuts rates on loans to other banks, it is hoped that the banks will pass this savings on to its customers through similar cuts on credit cards and loans.

The Fed incorporates its third monetary policy tool by adding to or reducing reserves, which is money banks set aside from deposits as a security measure. This is a way to make sure banks have enough money on hand to cover depositor activity, such as making withdrawals and writing checks on their accounts.

US banks, including the Fed, are required to keep a percentage, or a fraction, of their total deposits in reserve. Money above and beyond the reserve requirement is available for lending, which stimulates the economy. To make sure this happens, the Fed may reduce the reserve rate requirement. So, if a bank has deposits equaling $1 million and the reserve rate is 20 percent, the reserve of cash that would have to be on hand would be $200,000. At a lower reserve rate of 10 percent, only $100,000 has to be held in reserve. The extra $100,000 deposited in the bank is now freed up for lending and the eventual spending or investing that will strengthen an economy.

Keeping Prices Affordable

Good economic policy can help shorten a recession and ease the problems associated with a slowdown. Bad economic policy, however, can actually bring on a recession. One example of the latter type of policy involves price controls.

Price controls are a legal limit on how high prices in a certain business sector can rise. The limit is also called a cap. Governments have used price controls frequently in the past to fight inflation. At first glance, it would seem that any policy aimed at keeping prices affordable would be a good thing. While price controls may help in the short term, they can disrupt the business cycle.

The reason has to do with the effect that fixing prices at a set amount has on production. Placing a cap on the price of a good or service keeps the cost low for consumers, which increases demand. As a result, businesses need more workers and materials to keep up with the increased demand. However, when price controls are in place, companies are not able to set higher prices that let them make a profit after increased expenses. Without that profit, they can't afford new employees or other higher production costs associated with increased production.

Eventually, these companies lose money. They either go out of business or switch to providing goods and services that don't have price controls and that allow them to make a healthy profit. Either way, the supply of the original price-controlled item decreases, even though demand from the public is still high. This negatively affects the natural flow of supply and demand, by imposing prices and quantities that are most likely not reflective of the true market forces.

Personal Policy Measures

We've seen how governments handle a recession through economic policy. Now let's take a look at some personal policy measures you can take that will help you cope with an economic slowdown. While there's no way to become absolutely recession-proof, there are commonsense steps that you can take to protect your wealth and purchasing power.

Getting out of debt is the smartest thing you can do to fight the effects of a recession. Owing money is a huge drain on your finances. Pay as much as you can on your monthly credit card statement, not just the minimum. That way you avoid paying extra interest and other fees associated with carrying your debt from one month to the next.

Staying out of debt in the first place is also wise, so scale back on your spending. First, put yourself on a budget. This can be done on a monthly basis. Figure out how much money you bring home each month, after taxes. Then calculate how much you spend on necessities such as food, bills, and rent. Since some of these expenses will vary from month to month, you can add them and get an average. Once you write this information down, find areas of your budget that you can cut. Maybe you can eat at home more often, and you can rent movies instead of going to the cinema. In the areas where you must spend, such as food and gas, spend wisely. Be on the lookout for sales and the lowest prices, and take advantage of all discounts or rebates offered by manufacturers.

Additional Protections

What you do with the money you don't spend is just as important as budgeting the money you plan to spend. Open a savings account and put money

During a recession, being in debt can be a real burden. Try to whittle down your debt by paying as much as you can on each month's credit card statement and only using your card when absolutely necessary.

Digital Age Effects

Electronic devices and social media offer clues about the economy. With a few strokes of your fingers you can read news items, stock quotes, financial advice, economists' predictions, and other material.

Twitter, Facebook, LinkedIn, Instagram, and other social media sites let users air concerns about layoffs, pay cuts, foreclosures, and other issues. In a recession, people need help meeting needs. Social giving "campaigns"—also known as crowdfunding—allow people to give money to help friends and strangers. Common reasons include property loss caused by fire or weather, chronic illness, and unexpected death.

The term *crowdfunding* was the brainchild of William Sullivan (left) and Kate Curran. Sullivan first used it on his blog, fundavlog. With crowdfunding, people can donate to help people in need.

into it as often as you can. Try to find one with a high interest rate that will allow your savings to grow steadily over time. Your savings can act as an emergency fund if you find yourself out of a job or otherwise struggling with cash during a recession. You can even take saving a step further by opening an IRA, which is a retirement account. Believe it or not, it's never too early to think about retirement and your financial future.

You can also make a few investments. A recession can be a good time to invest because the price of stocks and bonds is generally lower, which makes them easier to buy. This is sometimes referred to on Wall Street as bargain shopping. When the economy rebounds and starts to expand and stock prices begin to rise again, you are likely to earn money on your investment.

Speak with your parents, an economics professor, or a financial adviser to find out more about IRAs and investing. Safer investments usually involve long-established, financially sound companies that produce products or services that are likely to remain in demand for a long time, during both economic good and bad times. These companies should also be putting a lot of their money and energy into research and development, signaling that they intend to stay at the leading edge of their industries.

Unemployment runs high during a recession, so if you don't already have a job, you may find it tough to get one. There are fewer jobs available when production is down. Consequently, not only will you have competition from others who are your own age, you may also be up against adults who have more experience but have been laid off because of the slowdown.

Get creative when trying to find work during a recession. Instead of holding out for your dream job, take a position that will let you progress to your ideal once the economy gets better. Think about part-time employment or starting your own business. Seek help from friends and family in finding leads in the field of your choice.

Creativity and patience aren't just helpful when trying to find work. Those traits, along with careful financial planning and industriousness, will help you get through even the longest lasting recessions. Stay flexible, work hard, save money in safe places, and spend carefully. If you do so, you will be well positioned to roar back into financial life once the economy turns around again.

CHAPTER 6
What's Next?

One of the first steps of dealing with the effects of a recession is the acknowledgment that they are inevitable. By the middle of 2015, experts hinted at the possibility of a new recession. The news is never good.

Understanding what a recession is and how it works enables us to better appreciate that recession is a normal component of the business cycle. Like other aspects, a recession offers valuable lifelong lessons and the opportunity to acquire life skills that can be applied whether the economy turns up or down.

Expect the unexpected is one lesson gleaned from the Great Recession. During the official eighteen months of its duration, the recession dramatically impacted every sector of the economy. That was expected, given the nature of recessions. What was unexpected was the crippling impact on families' financial affairs. Particularly troubling was people's inabilities to find work in their career fields, forcing many to take jobs at annual salaries significantly lower than their pre–Great Recession employment.

Flexibility is a life skill. In any economy flexible workers will always find it easier to gain and keep employment. A willingness to learn a new job skill at a current employer shines the spotlight on your flexibility and may increase your job prospects.

Supply and demand are a mainstay of every economy. When times are good few people worry about whether there will be sufficient supplies of mainstay staples like bread, milk, and water—or even gasoline for cars, farming equipment, or business vehicles. Saving takes a backseat to spending and investing. The Great Recession revealed how easily demand outpaces supply during a recession, resulting in skyrocketed prices. Grocery shopping becomes tougher as consumers make critical decisions about a family's true needs. Throughout the United States, consumers decried the price of gasoline, often forgoing purchases or buying less gasoline and opting to utilize public transportation rather than ride to work.

One life skill that helps in an economic downturn is a focus on the future. But, this focus rarely originates during a recession. It is demonstrated by a commitment to saving and living within your means. It incorporates paying bills.

Paying Bills

Cities, governments, companies, families, and individuals regularly generate bills that help pump money into various sectors of the economy. Paying those assures an economically sound future.

For personal expenditures, household utilities, rent or mortgage payments, transportation costs, and other everyday items generate bills that require monthly, quarterly, or annual payments. Paying those bills during a tough economy may prove challenging. Not paying them increases financial stress and may result in short-term utility shutoffs, eviction, foreclosure, or other devastating economic consequences.

Being fiscally responsible starts long before a recession hits or even before you become accountable for bill paying. A commonsense approach to paying bills is to know what you owe. How much do you owe for each regular household or personal expense? Knowing those exact figures will help you better prepare a spending plan—budget—to pay them. Thanks to electronic billing you can receive statements via e-mail and a notification when your bill due date is approaching.

"Pay before you play" is a second effective way to handle bills. This strategy encourages bill payment before you spend money on nonessential purchases such as movies, fast food meals, entertainment (including music, videos, and books), or vacations. Setting up automatic payments to the payee lets you set the due date, helping you avoid missed or late payments.

"Go for low" is a third way to pay bills. How many TV channels can you watch at one time? Do you really use that much cell phone data each month? Do you need a monthly subscription to an online or print publication? Is that service agreement provided in another household contract you already have? It is easy to rack up extra fees by adding services that sound good but which cause an affordable item to be less so over time. So, ask yourself, "Do I really need that?" If the answer is no, find out how to remove that extra charge on your next bill or during a contract renewal. The lower your expense, the greater the possibility you may be able to pay it during a recession.

"Face the facts" is a final way for you to reduce your monthly costs. If you struggle to pay bills, ask for help. If your ability to pay your bills is affected by downsizing, unemployment, or a salary freeze, don't delay; call your various payees and determine how you can modify your payments. If you consistently pay your utility bills on time you may also be eligible for a "budget plan" that offers a lower, set fee each month that prevents bill hikes caused by fluctuations based on usage or weather.

Apps are right at your fingertips all the time with a smartphone. Why not use one to help keep your budget in check during a recession, even your coffee purchases?

You will owe bills as long as you use services to meet needs. The sooner you learn to handle those responsibly, the easier it may be for you to thrive during a recession.

There's an App for That

Use apps on your smartphone, tablet, or laptop to learn more about recession or other issues affecting the economy. Some apps cover more technical topics specific to the economy and how it works. Personal finance apps are more user friendly, providing information on spending, budgeting, and investing. Apps you may learn from now and use later include mortgage calculators, debt reduction calculators, and currency convertors.

Another Recession?

Is the United States headed for another recession any time soon? The answer to that question varies, depending on the economic experts polled, as indicators seemed to offer a mixed bag of results in 2015. Even if the time frame is uncertain, we know from our study on recession that economic downturns are inevitable parts of the business cycle and it is therefore best to prepare now.

Timeline of US Recessions

1819 First major depression in America and panic of 1819.

1918 Recession follows end of World War I.

1929 Great Depression begins.

July 1953–May 1954 Recession.

August 1957–April 1958 Recession.

November 1973–March 1975 Recession sparked by international political disagreements.

Late 1980s–Early 1990s Banking crisis: many savings and loan banks close.

October 19, 1987 Blue Monday: the stock market experiences one of largest single-day drops in US history.

1990–91 Decrease in manufacturing production spurs recession.

2001 First twenty-first century recession: the technology stock bubble bursts, and 9/11 shock impacts economy.

December 2007 Great Recession begins. Risky subprime mortgages contribute to start of Great Recession, which lasts until June 2009.

Bibliographic Sources

Bair, Sheila. *The Bullies of Wall Street: This Is How Greed Messed Up Our Economy*. New York, NY: Simon & Schuster Children's Publishing Division, 2015.

Board of Governors of the Federal Reserve System. "In the Shadow of the Great Recession: Experiences and Perspectives of Young Workers." Board of Governors of the Federal Reserve System, November 2014. Retrieved May 2015 (http://www.federalreserve.gov/econresdata/2013-experiences-and-perspectives-of-young-workers-201411.pdf)

Bureau of Economic Analysis, US Department of Commerce. "Measuring the Economy: A Primer on GDP and the National Income and Product Accounts." Bureau of Economic Analysis, US Department of Commerce, October 2014. Retrieved June 2015 (http://www.bea.gov/national/pdf/nipa_primer.pdf).

Council of Economic Advisers. "15 Economic Facts About Millennials." Council of Economic Advisers, October 2014. Retrieved June 2015 (https://www.whitehouse.gov/sites/default/files/docs/millennials_report.pdf).

Novack, Janet, and Samantha Sharf. "The Recession Generation: How Millennials Are Changing Money Management Forever." Forbes, July 30, 2014. Retrieved June 2015 (http://www.forbes.com/sites/

samanthasharf/2014/07/30/the-recession-generation-how-millennials-are-changing-money-management-forever/).

US Bureau of Labor Statistics. "The Recession of 2007–2009." US Bureau of Labor Statistics, February 2012. Retrieved May 2015 (http://www.bls.gov/spotlight/2012/recession/)

Wiltz, Teresa. "Q&A: How the Great Recession Affected Children." The Pew Charitable Trusts, March 17, 2015. Retrieved May 2015 (http://www.pewtrusts.org/en/research-and-analysis/blogs/stateline/2015/3/17/qa-how-the-great-recession-affected-children).

Glossary

bubble—In economics, a rapid rise in price and value.

business cycle—The natural way the economy works, through a series of ups (expansions) and downs (contractions).

central bank—A country's primary money authority.

circulation—Currency moving freely through the economy; cash distributed to the public.

countercyclic—Moving in the opposite direction of the business cycle.

crowdfunding—A fund-raiser to help people in tough times, usually conducted online.

default—To fail to satisfy a commitment, such as a loan.

depression—A period of very low economic activity; a severe recession.

domino effect—When one event sets off a chain of similar events, like lined-up dominoes that knock each other over.

downsize—When a business reduces staff to save costs. Also describes a person's efforts to reduce his or her possessions to reduce debt or simplify life.

economic indicators—Data and statistics that indicate, or point out, the direction the economy is taking.

economic shocks—Unpredictable events that affect the economy from the outside.

embargo—A ban on trade, import or export, with a particular country.

exports—Goods and services a country sells to other nations.

foreclose—To take control of a property after the person holding the mortgage fails to make payments.

globalization—The development of connections between businesses and marketplaces around the world.

gross domestic product (GDP)—The total value of all goods and services produced in the country in a given period of time, such as a month, a quarter (three months), or a year.

gross national product (GNP)—The total amount of goods and services produced in a country over a given time period.

gross world product (GWP)—The total amount of all goods and services produced throughout the world over a given time period.

imports—Goods and services that a country buys from other nations.

inflation—A rise in the price level of goods and services.

interest—The extra amount of cash paid as a sort of fee or service charge to the lender when money is borrowed. The interest charged is usually a certain percentage of the total loan amount.

lagging—Falling behind.

menu costs—The expenses associated with reprinting materials that list the prices of a business's offerings to reflect changes in the economy and rising costs.

Millennials—People who are eighteen to thirty-four years old.

mortgage—A loan taken out against the value of your home (or other property). If the loan is not repaid in the set amount of time, the lender takes ownership of your home.

negative growth—A decrease in the number of goods and services a country can produce over a given time period.

payee—The recipient of a cash or electronic payment.

peak—The top point to which an economy expands during a business cycle.

positive growth—An increase in the number of goods and services a country can produce over a given time period.

procyclic—Moving in the same direction as the business cycle.

ration—A limit on the amount of a good that consumers may buy, usually established and enforced by the government during times of shortage.

recession—When the economy experiences a slowdown, or contraction.

salary freeze—When a person's salary is not increased for a certain amount of time.

slowdown—A decrease in the rate of consumer spending and production of goods.

speculators—Those making risky investments in an attempt to make a quick profit.

stagnation—When the economy shows no sign of moving down or up.

sticky wages—Wages that can't change as quickly as the business cycle.

subprime loan—A loan to a borrower with a weak credit history.

subsidy—Money given to an industry, by the government, to offset the cost of producing goods.

supply and demand—A natural law that maps out how buyers and sellers act on their own and react to each other.

trough—The lowest point to which an economy contracts during a business cycle.

Further Reading

Books

Bair, Sheila. *The Bullies of Wall Street: This Is How Greed Messed Up Our Economy*. New York, NY: Simon & Schuster Children's Publishing Division, 2015.

Bianchi, David W. *Blue Chip Kids: What Every Child (and Parent) Should Know About Money, Investing, and the Stock Market*. Hoboken, NJ: Wiley, 2015.

Christen, Carol, and Richard N. Bolles *What Color Is Your Parachute? for Teens, Third Edition: Discover Yourself, Design Your Future, and Plan for Your Dream Job*, 3rd edition. New York, NY: Ten Speed Press, 2015.

Donovan, Sandy. *Budgeting Smarts: How to Set Goals, Save Money, Spend Wisely, and More*. Minneapolis, Minn.: Lerner Publications, 2012.

Hulick, Kathryn. *The Economics of a Video Game* (Economics of Entertainment). New York, NY: Crabtree Publishing Company, 2014.

Kishtainy, Niall. *The Economics Book* (Big Ideas Simply Explained). London: DK Publishing, 2014.

McGuire, Kara. *The Teen Money Manual: A Guide to Cash, Credit, Spending, Saving, Work, Wealth, and More*. Mankato, Minn.: Capstone Young Readers, 2014.

Websites

Bank of Canada
www.bank-banque-canada.ca
As the country's central bank, the Bank of Canada is responsible for the national financial system, including monetary policy, bank notes, and fund management.

Board of Governors of the Federal Reserve System
www.federalreserve.gov
The Federal Reserve System is the central bank of the United States.

BizKids
bizkids.com/blog
Information about handling finances for kids.

Council for Economic Education
www.councilforeconed.org/
Through programs and publications, the CEE helps students think and choose responsibly as consumers, savers, investors, citizens, members of the workforce, and effective participants in a global economy.

Federal Reserve Bank of St. Louis
www.stlouisfed.org/topics/topics-in-the-news/great-recession
Federal Reserve Bank of St. Louis' website page with information on the Great Recession.

History and Purpose of the Fed

www.stlouisfed.org/in-plain-english/history-and-purpose-of-the-fed

Federal Reserve Board's educational website of videos and written material.

The State of Working America

stateofworkingamerica.org

A publication that addresses economic trends of the Economic Policy Institute's publication on economic trends.

US Department of the Treasury

www.ustreas.gov

The Treasury Department is the executive agency responsible for promoting economic prosperity and ensuring the financial security of the United States.

Index